# BASIC / NOT BORING
# LANGUAGE SKILLS

# STUDY & RESEARCH

## Grades 6–8+

Inventive Exercises to Sharpen
Skills and Raise Achievement

Series Concept & Development
by Imogene Forte & Marjorie Frank
Exercises by Joy MacKenzie

Incentive Publications, Inc.
Nashville, Tennessee

*About the cover:*
Bound resist, or tie dye, is the most ancient known method
of fabric surface design. The brilliance of the basic tie dye
design on this cover reflects the possibilities that emerge
from the mastery of basic skills.

*Illustrated by Kathleen Bullock*
*Cover art by Mary Patricia Deprez, dba Tye Dye Mary®*
*Cover design by Marta Drayton, Joe Shibley, and W. Paul Nance*
*Edited by Anna Quinn*

ISBN 0-86530-363-0

PRINTED IN THE UNITED STATES OF AMERICA

# TABLE OF CONTENTS

# CELEBRATE BASIC
# STUDY & RESEARCH SKILLS

Basic does not mean boring! There certainly is nothing dull about turning into a snooping, sleuthing detective and . . .

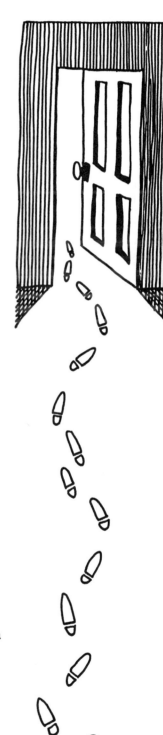

    . . . tracking down notorious criminals hiding in cities around the globe

    . . . investigating a tip left by an anonymous phone caller

    . . . solving some mysteries about the letter "Z"

    . . . searching for answers to dilemmas in a cemetery

    . . . following an old map to find buried treasure

    . . . gathering important evidence from a crime scene

    . . . figuring out which suspect stole the royal jewels

    . . . getting to know some famous real and fictional sleuths

    . . . searching for the truth about a disappearing ship

    . . . exposing the true identity of a bunch of fugitive criminals

    . . . deciding if evidence proves that an "accident" was not really accidental

The idea of celebrating the basics is just what it sounds like—enjoying and developing the basic study and research skills. The pages that follow are full of exercises for students that will help to review and strengthen specific, basic skills that will help them learn and study information in all content areas. This is not just another ordinary "fill-in-the-blanks" way to learn. The high-interest activities will put students to work applying a rich variety of the most important study and research skills while solving challenging detective "cases" which make use of their skills.

The pages in this book can be used in many ways:
- for individual students to sharpen a particular skill
- with a small group needing to relearn or strengthen a skill
- as an instructional tool for teaching a skill to any size group
- by students working on their own
- by students working under the direction of an adult

**Each page may be used to introduce a new skill, reinforce a skill, or assess a student's ability to perform a skill.** And, there's more than just the 40+ pages of great student activities! You'll also find a hearty appendix of resources helpful for students and teachers—including a ready-to-use test on these study and research skills.

As students take on the challenges of these adventures with grammar and usage, they will grow in their mastery of basic skills and will enjoy learning to the fullest. And as you watch them check off the study and research skills they've strengthened, you can celebrate with them!

# SKILLS CHECKLIST FOR STUDY & RESEARCH

| ✔ | SKILL | PAGE(S) |
|---|-------|---------|
| | Listen to get information | 10 |
| | Understand and follow directions | 10, 16, 17 |
| | Find and put words in alphabetical order | 11 |
| | Use a table of contents to find information | 12, 13 |
| | Use an index to find information | 14, 15 |
| | Find information on copyright pages | 18 |
| | Use a dictionary or glossary to find word meanings | 11, 19 |
| | Use a thesaurus to find words for a specific purpose | 20 |
| | Use and draw maps to find and show locations and information | 16, 17 |
| | Use an atlas to find information | 21, 22 |
| | Use an encyclopedia to find information | 11, 22, 23, 24, 30 |
| | Use an encyclopedia index | 25 |
| | Use a reader's guide to locate information | 26 |
| | Use an almanac to find information | 27, 28 |
| | Use a biographical dictionary to find information | 29 |
| | Use a literary reference book to find information | 30 |
| | Find information in *The Guinness Book of World Records* | 31 |
| | Locate sections and information in a newspaper | 32 |
| | Use and create a bibliography to gather source information | 33 |
| | Select the best resource for a task | 34, 35, 36 |
| | Find and interpret information from charts and tables | 37 |
| | Find and interpret information from a graph | 38 |
| | Find and interpret information from a diagram | 39 |
| | Find and interpret information from a timeline | 40 |
| | Gain information by careful observation | 41, 43, 44, 45 |
| | Form questions to gain information | 42 |
| | Find and organize information to give a report | 44 |
| | Use scanning and skimming to gain information quickly | 46, 47 |
| | Organize information by outlining | 46, 48 |
| | Summarize information to use or study | 46, 49, 50 |
| | Be familiar with and use the Dewey Decimal System | 51 |
| | Use a card catalog or on-line catalog to find books | 52 |

# STUDY & RESEARCH

## Skills Exercises

# STOLEN JEWELS!

A priceless emerald necklace is missing from the safe of a European monarchy. One of these wily characters below has taken it. Find out who. Here's how:

Cut this page on the dotted line. Give the bottom portion of the page to a friend and ask your friend to read the directions aloud to you, slowly and carefully, one at a time. Do only what the directions tell you to do. Do nothing that you are not told to do. Do not erase. Do not ask questions. Each direction may be read only one time. If you listen well, your answer should solve the mystery!

1  2  3  4  5  6  7  8  9  10  11  12  13  14  15  16  17  18  19  20  21  22  23  24  25  26

- - - - - - - - - - - - - - - - - - - - - - - - - - - - - - - - - - - - - - - - - - - - - -

DIRECTIONS: Read each direction clearly and carefully ONE time. Do not answer questions.

1. Put the letter next to the swami's feather in box 8.
2. Put the letter near the nose of the dog in boxes 3, 7, 13, and 26.
3. Put the letter on the ear of the convict in box 10.
4. Put the letter on the hat of the chef in box 14.
5. Put the letter on the hat of Sneak in boxes 1 and 17.
6. Put the letter next to the opera singer's earring in boxes 11 and 22.
7. Put the letter near the dog's ear in box 12.
8. Put the letter on the chef's chin in boxes 2 and 6.
9. Put the letter on the bald head in boxes 16, 19, and 25.
10. Put the letter on Sneak's lapel in box 20.
11. Put the letter at the end of the singer's nose in box 5.
12. Put the letter at the point of the swami's nose in box 24.

Name

# "Z" CONNECTION

Z has always been a somewhat mysterious letter. Be a smart sleuth and connect clues to solve "z" mysteries below.

I.  Use your dictionary and encyclopedia to complete "Z" connection between the "Z" words in Column A with their matching identification in Column B.

| A | B |
|---|---|
| 1. _____ Zedekiah | A. a Greek god |
| 2. _____ Zambezi | B. a North American Indian |
| 3. _____ Zimbabwe | C. a musical instrument |
| 4. _____ zither | D. a metallic element |
| 5. _____ zinc | E. a sea inlet |
| 6. _____ Zuider Zee | F. a river |
| 7. _____ Zagreb | G. a king |
| 8. _____ ziggurat | H. an imaginary zone in the heavens |
| 9. _____ zoonosis | I. a mineral rock |
| 10. _____ zoology | J. a disease humans get from animals |
| 11. _____ Zeus | K. a form of Buddhism |
| 12. _____ Zola | L. a study of animals |
| 13. _____ Zurich | M. capital of Croatia |
| 14. _____ Zircon | N. a pyramid |
| 15. _____ Zeppelin | O. a plant |
| 16. _____ Zen | P. an African country |
| 17. _____ Zanzibar | Q. a French novelist |
| 18. _____ Zapotec | R. a German scientist |
| 19. _____ zinnia | S. an island of Tanzania |
| 20. _____ zodiac | T. a city in Switzerland |

II.  Use the space below to write the "Z" words in alphabetical order.

| | |
|---|---|
| 1. _____ | 11. _____ |
| 2. _____ | 12. _____ |
| 3. _____ | 13. _____ |
| 4. _____ | 14. _____ |
| 5. _____ | 15. _____ |
| 6. _____ | 16. _____ |
| 7. _____ | 17. _____ |
| 8. _____ | 18. _____ |
| 9. _____ | 19. _____ |
| 10. _____ | 20. _____ |

Name _____

# MYSTERIES OF THE MIND

One of the most important mysteries you will ever need to solve is the mystery of how your mind works and what you can do to sharpen and assist its processes.

The table of contents on page 13 is taken from a book called *Learning to Learn* by Gloria Frender. The questions below will help you see how you could use this book to increase the efficiency of your brain power and your study skills. See if you can identify pages that will give you the best chance of success. Answer by recording the page numbers.

1.  If you wanted to identify the strengths and weaknesses of your study habits, what page(s) would you choose to read? _____

2.  What page(s) might help you become a better reader? _____

3.  If you have problems remembering what you study, on which page(s) might you find advice? _____

4.  If you were trying to improve your spelling study skills, which page(s) might supply some hints? _____

5.  You never know whether or not to guess on test questions. Which page(s) might answer this question? _____

6.  Where would you find advice on how to make a good study guide? _____

7.  Where would you look to gain understanding about how your mind learns? _____

8.  Whoops! You had a dental appointment and missed almost ½ day. You've got a test coming up and an assignment due. You don't have the information you need. What page(s) might help? _____

9.  It's hard to pay attention when the teacher lectures a long time. You're supposed to take notes, but how do you know what's important? And how can you listen so long? Help is on page(s) _____

10. If you want to be really great at getting information from charts and graphs, you might find some good pointers on page(s) _____

11. Test tomorrow? You didn't know? Ball game tonight? You're in deep trouble. Any pages here you might check out—quickly? _____

12. Several pages offer advice on dealing with main ideas. They are pages _____

Name _____

# TABLE OF CONTENTS

*Partial Table of Contents from* Learning To Learn *by Gloria Frender,© 1990, by Incentive Publications, Inc. Used by permission.*

# DETECTIVE'S DOWNTIME DILEMMA

Small-town detectives often have a block of slow days. A pleasant way to pass the time is to give attention to personal hobbies and interests. Detective Hyde has discovered a great book of activities that suit his interests—nature and the environment. Check the index on page 15 to determine on which pages Officer Hyde might find information about the following topics. List the pages he should check for each topic.

DIRT SCULPTURES?

1. How to grow fruit in a bottle _____

2. Making a necklace _____

3. How to do grave rubbings _____

4. Building bird houses _____

5. Making a backyard water slide _____

6. Holiday activities _____

7. Making dirt sculptures _____

8. Growing plants _____

9. Making weather instruments _____

10. How to dry a wedding bouquet for a keepsake _____

11. Making rain tea _____

12. Constructing a hideaway _____

13. Planning a party for the first day of spring _____

14. Making designs from shells _____

15. How to fry an egg on a sidewalk _____

16. Choosing tools for nature activities _____

17. Ideas for things to make for a party table (other than food) _____

18. How to make jelly _____

19. Games to play after dark _____

20. How to make a talisman (You may need a dictionary to help you find this one!) _____

Name _____

*Partial Index from* Puddles & Wings & Grapevine Swings *by Imogene Forte & Marjorie Frank,*
©1982, Incentive Publications, Inc. Used by permission.

Name

# HIDDEN TREASURE HINTS

An anonymous tip has led you to an uncharted island in the Caribbean Sea, where you have located a cave filled with human skeletons and rotting wooden chests. Among the debris, you find an old book which you discover to be a diary. You are able to decipher portions of its last entry . . .

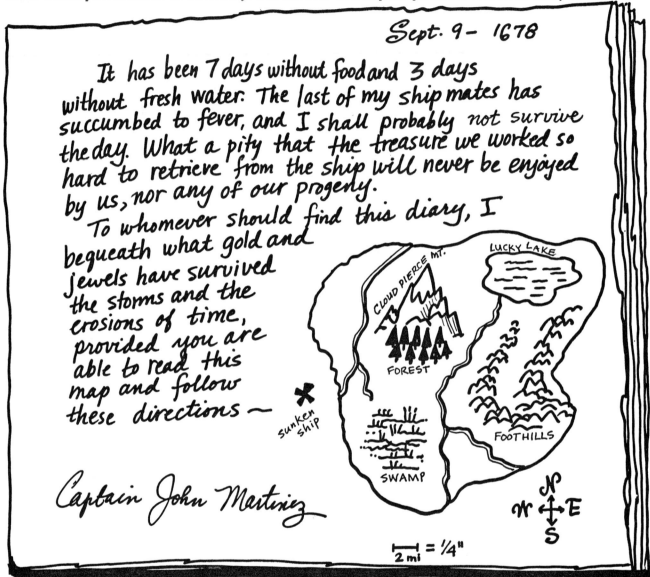

Sept. 9 - 1678

It has been 7 days without food and 3 days without fresh water. The last of my ship mates has succumbed to fever, and I shall probably not survive the day. What a pity that the treasure we worked so hard to retrieve from the ship will never be enjoyed by us, nor any of our progeny.

To whomever should find this diary, I bequeath what gold and jewels have survived the storms and the erosions of time, provided you are able to read this map and follow these directions —

Captain John Martinez

sunken ship

CLOUD PIERCE MT.

LUCKY LAKE

FOREST

FOOTHILLS

SWAMP

2 mi = 1/4"

DIRECTIONS: Begin at the wreck of the Sarasota. Travel directly toward land to the mouth of the west fork of the river. Follow this river fork upstream 4 miles to the split of the rivers. Head directly east through the forest which is at the base of a mountain. Go 10 miles and you will hit another river. Follow this river north for 4 miles. Then turn east and walk 4 miles. You will be at the mouth of a valley between two ranges of hills. Travel south for 8 miles between the ranges of hills until you hit the foothills at the south end of the valley. As soon as you hit the foothills, on the southeast edge of the valley, you will find treasure.

Trace your journey on the map Captain John has sketched.

Name _____

# DANGEROUS IMPULSE

Would you ordinarily laugh at someone who claims to know where hidden treasure is buried? Maybe you would, but today, a mysterious phone call jump-started your curiosity. The strange voice at the other end of the line gave you these directions for finding a hidden treasure, and your impulse was to follow the directions to the treasure—or, perhaps, to danger!

Read the entire set of directions carefully before you touch a pencil. Look at the compass on the map; then draw a map that will help you picture exactly where the treasure may be. Draw your map in the space below.

DIRECTIONS: Leave your driveway at sundown. Turn left on Beech Road. After you cross the creek, take the second road on your right. Travel exactly one mile directly south. Then turn left at the old graveyard. Go over the railroad tracks and take the right fork at the grove of trees. Turn left at the first road and follow the black rail fence southeast to the lake. Park by the old cabin and wait for further direction.

Name

# COPYRIGHT = NO COPYCATS

Often, clues to mysteries are found in the most unlikely places. A good detective must know how to look for information in unusual places. On this page, you will find information from the copyright pages from six different books. You may be surprised by the things you can learn from these pages. Careful reading of the pages will help you answer the questions below. Before you begin, look up the word **copyright** in a dictionary or encyclopedia.

1. What is a copyright? _____

2. How long is a copyright effective? _____

3. Which books have a copyright owned by a company? _____

4. Which copyright is most recent? _____

5. Who is the owner of the copyright for *What Every Teenager Should Know?* _____

6. Which books were printed out of the United States? _____

7. Which book has illustrations copyrighted by someone other than the author? _____

8. Who is the publisher of *How to Exercise without Lifting a Finger?* _____

9. Which is the earliest copyright? _____

10. Which book gives some permission to reprint pages? _____

---

Math in the Real World of Architecture
Author: Shirley Cook
©1996 by Incentive Publications, Inc.
Publisher: Incentive Publications, Inc., Nashville, TN
Printed in the United States
Pages labeled with the statement © 1996 Incentive Publications, Inc., Nashville, TN are intended for reproduction. Permission is hereby granted to the purchaser of one copy of Math in the Real World of Architecture to reproduce these pages in sufficient quantities for meeting the purchaser's own classroom needs.

---

Brothers and Other Annoyances
Author: Henry Q. Henry, III
©1990 by Bretsone Publishing Co.
Publisher: Bretstone Publishing Co., NY, NY
Printed in Singapore

---

Training Your Pet Python
Author: J. S. Reptile
©1982 by J. S. Reptile; illus. by A. Copper Head
Publisher: Zoo Press, Chicago, IL
Printed in Australia

---

How to Exercise Without Lifting A Finger
Author: Russell L. Bow
©1989 by Russell L. Bow
Publisher: Bodyworks Press, Inc., Philadelphia, PA
Printed in the United States

---

What Every Teenager Should Know
Author: Dr. I. Noahtall
©1983 by Dr. I. Noahtall
Publisher; J. C. Landover, Inc., Wichita, Kansas
Printed in the United States

---

Tales That Twist Your Tongue
Author: Samantha Cynthia Simms-Smith
©1992 by Samantha Cynthia Simms-Smith
Publisher: C. C. Cooper, Inc., San Francisco, CA
Printed in Hong Kong

---

Name _____

# BLACK AND BLUE

Black and blue is what a sleuth becomes if he or she is not very careful. There are all kinds of black and blue things in our world—some good, some bad. See if you can match each of these blacks and blues with the correct definition. A dictionary and an encyclopedia may help!

_____ 1. blue chip

_____ 2. blue blood

_____ 3. Black Forest

_____ 4. Black Beauty

_____ 5. Blackmun, Harry A.

_____ 6. black hole

_____ 7. blue bonnet

_____ 8. black stump

_____ 9. blue gum

_____ 10. black box

_____ 11. Black Prince

_____ 12. black buck

_____ 13. blueprint

_____ 14. black widow

_____ 15. Black Sea

_____ 16. Blackfoot

_____ 17. blue laws

_____ 18. blacklist

_____ 19. Blue Ridge

_____ 20. blackmail

_____ 21. Black Monday

_____ 22. blues

_____ 23. bluegrass

_____ 24. black magic

_____ 25. Bluebeard

A. a folk tale character who murdered six wives

B. a harmful female spider

C. a criminal offense of extortion

D. stock market crash of October, 1987

E. mountainous wooded region of West Germany

F. member of a Plains American Indian tribe

G. melancholy African American music

H. an antelope of India

I. inland body of water in Southeast Europe

J. name for a unit containing flight recorders

K. Kentucky pasture for horses

L. Colonial New England rules enforcing morals

M. to ban or boycott

N. a Texas flowering plant

O. Australian trees

P. a place in space from which nothing escapes

Q. a stock that sells at a high price

R. story of a horse's life

S. a person of noble or aristocratic descent

T. a range of mountains extending from West Virginia to Georgia

U. U.S. Supreme Court justice, appointed 1970

V. photographic process used in engineering

W. voodoo, witchcraft

X. Prince of Wales—eldest son of King Edward III

Y. an imaginary boundary between civilization and the Australian outback

Name _____

# TRIPLE-A DETECTIVES

### BORK
Affable
Authoritative
Absentminded

### SHARK
Aggressive
Audacious
Agile

### JESS
Adventurous
Ardent
Alert

_____   _____   _____

_____   _____   _____

_____   _____   _____

_____   _____   _____

_____   _____   _____

    Bork, Shark, and Jess are the three members of the Triple-A Detective Agency. Each has a distinct set of characteristics that make him or her a superb sleuth. Bork is affable, authoritative, and absentminded; Shark is aggressive, audacious, and agile; and Jess is ever adventurous, ardent, and alert. Together, they are unstoppable. Look carefully at the portrait of each detective and add at least **five** additional character traits you guess from each picture.

    Use your thesaurus to locate another word that is a synonym for each "A" word listed AND for each of your own word choices. Try to choose words that make these three appear to be a clever, fascinating trio.

Name _____

# "B"EELINE TO OBLIVION

| | | | |
|---|---|---|---|
| Bahamas | Bahrain | Bangladesh | Benin |
| Barbados | Budapest | Belize | Bhutan |
| Boston | Botswana | Brazil | Boise |
| Bulgaria | Burundi | Birmingham | Belgium |

When a criminal is trying to hide from authorities, she tries to locate a place in the world where she is unlikely to be easily found. After you have used an atlas or other resources to answer the following questions, decide which of the above "B" places on the globe you think would be the best hiding place and tell why.

1. Circle in the list above each word that does not name a nation.

2. Find an island, not listed above, which is located in the Baltic Sea.

3. Which is located closest to the equator?
   British Isles       Baku
   Brazzaville        Broome

4. Which city has the highest elevation?
   Boston       Beirut
   Belgrade     Bogotá

5. Which city has the lowest population?
   Baffin Island      Bali
   Borneo             Budapest

6. Which is NOT a capital city?
   Bucharest       Bern       Birmingham       Baghdad

7. Which country's border touches the Black Sea?
   Bulgaria       Belize       Brazil       Burundi

8. Which is located farthest inland from an ocean or sea?
   Broken Hill       Bandjarmasin       Bergen       Bhutan

9. Which two cities are closest together?
   Bratislava & Budapest       Brazilia & Beliz       Barcelona & Birmingham

10. Which city is located closest to the Sea of Galilee?
    Brussels       Beirut       Berlin       Bordeaux

11. For a real criminal, I think _____ would be the best hiding place because

_____

_____

_____ .

Name _____

# MISS WATSON IS MISSING!

A young woman is missing, and the only clue to her existence is a suitcase found in San Francisco, bearing the name of Miss Jane Watson. You have been authorized by the FBI to open this bag and try to see if it contains any clues to Miss Watson's whereabouts. It is believed that Miss Watson may have left Boston, Massachusetts two to three weeks ago on a cross-country trip by car, train, and plane to San Francisco. She is known to have been a habitual buyer of souvenirs and it is unlikely that she would pass through any state or major city without securing at least one piece of memorabilia from each place she visited.

As you sort through the items in her luggage, try to determine the origin of each possession and place its number on the map to mark the place each was likely obtained. Perhaps as you mark the map, you will be able to trace Miss Watson's journey from Boston to San Francisco or whatever her last stop may have been. (A U. S. atlas and an encyclopedia will be useful tools for your investigation.)

Name

# MYSTERIES—UNSOLVED AND OTHERWISE

What's mysterious about a fish, an island, a triangle, a blue book? Find out! Each of these persons, places, or things has some connection to the world of mystery. Use your encyclopedias to help you explain the "mystery" factor of each item listed.

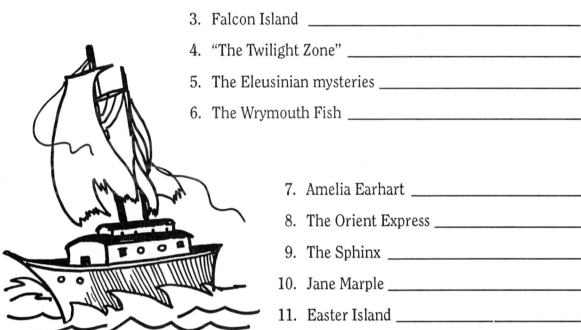

1. Hercule Poirot _____

2. Wormholes _____

3. Falcon Island _____

4. "The Twilight Zone" _____

5. The Eleusinian mysteries _____

6. The Wrymouth Fish _____

7. Amelia Earhart _____

8. The Orient Express _____

9. The Sphinx _____

10. Jane Marple _____

11. Easter Island _____

12. The Flying Dutchman _____

13. Mike Hammer _____

14. Henrik Ibsen _____

15. The Condon Report _____

16. The Bermuda Triangle _____

17. The Dead Sea Scrolls _____

18. The Mary Celeste _____

19. Project Blue Book _____

20. Francois Couperin _____

Name _____

# TORTURES, TOMBS, AND OTHER TRIVIA

The encyclopedia is full of wonderful curiosities. It's your job, detective, to track down these fourteen today.

1. Who threatened to torture Galileo?
   a) a police officer    b) his wife    c) a monk    d) a thief

2. What would you find in Scotland Yard?
   a) a garbage dump   b) tombs of famous people   c) criminal investigators   d) prizewinning roses

3. Where might you meet a white dwarf and a red giant?
   a) at a circus    b) in the galaxy    c) at a major league baseball game    d) in a fairy tale

4. If you had met Jim Jarratt, which of these would he probably be wearing?
   a) a suit of mail       c) a deep-sea diver's suit
   b) a space suit         d) a priest's robe

5. You've just had lunch with Tutankhamun. You've dined with . . .
   a) a tarantula   b) a Chinese emperor   c) a mountain   d) a mummy

6. Who was with Uri Gagarin on April 13, 1961?
   a) the Russian army    b) a monkey    c) a ballerina    d) no one

7. You watched Dr. John S. Pemberton at his work. What was he doing?
   a) drinking Coca Cola®         c) performing brain surgery
   b) examining fish              d) floating in space

8. When you're inspecting croup, what are you looking at?
   a) a government overthrow      d) the rear end of a horse
   b) a group of engineers        e) c and d
   c) an inflamed larynx

9. How long did William Henry Harrison serve as president of the United States?
   a) 1 month            b) 1 year            c) 7 years            d) not at all

10. If you're in the Marianas Trench, where are you?
    a) in a New York City sewer ditch          c) in the lowest spot of the ocean
    b) in a pit on a World War II battlefield   d) in a whale's mouth

11. Where are the Isles of Langerhans?
    a) in the North Sea      b) in your pancreas    c) on the moon's surface   d) in the Sea of Japan

12. What do you weigh on a Richter Scale?
    a) vegetables    b) elephants    c) earthquakes   d) diamonds

13. What would you do with a scul?
    a) give it to the police                  c) row it on a lake
    b) chop it onto a salad                    d) put it on a leash

14. You're in Tunguska, Siberia, in 1908, and you've been hit by something. What is it?
    a) a meteorite                             c) a UFO
    b) the worst avalanche of the century      d) the Black Death

Name

24

# INFORMATION FRENZY

Your assignment, Super Sleuth, should you elect (or be forced) to accept it, is to 1) locate the index volume of a set of encyclopedias and 2) use it to decide in which volume you will find the most complete information about the following. (Some topics may be addressed in more than one volume.)

| TOPIC | VOLUME LETTER(S) OR NUMBER(S) | PAGE #'S |
|---|---|---|
| 1. Hurricane warnings | | |
| 2. Capital city of Austria | | |
| 3. Picture of Alexander Hamilton | | |
| 4. Shakespeare's play, *Hamlet* | | |
| 5. A cottonmouth snake | | |
| 6. Seminole Indian wars | | |
| 7. The Goliath frog | | |
| 8. The Mormon Tabernacle in Utah | | |
| 9. How to set a dinner table | | |
| 10. The poisonous plant water hemlock | | |
| 11. Equipment for sky surfing | | |
| 12. Dr. Seuss | | |
| 13. How to give artificial respiration | | |
| 14. Ball lightning | | |
| 15. Habitats of vultures | | |
| 16. The Golden Gate Bridge | | |
| 17. What you do with a skeeter boat | | |
| 18. Who invented Sunday school? | | |
| 19. What's meant by "skin of teeth"? | | |
| 20. Bang's disease | | |
| 21. Merlin, the magician | | |

Name

# FUTURE FORECAST

Will detectives and law enforcement agencies still be around in the distant future? Use a *Reader's Guide to Periodicals* to find articles in which writers have made predictions about living in the twenty-first century. For the topics listed below, find at least one quote in a periodical that states an opinion or makes a prediction about that area of life in future years. Then give your own opinion or prediction in answer to the question in each category.

• FAMILY LIFE Quote: _____

_____

_____ Source: _____

Will you have larger or smaller families than your parents? _____

• JOBS Quote: _____

_____

_____ Source: _____

What new jobs might be created? _____

_____

• EDUCATION Quote: _____

_____

_____ Source: _____

Describe a feature of a future school your children may attend. _____

_____

_____

• HEALTH CARE Quote: _____

_____

_____

Source: _____

How will you likely be taken care of when you are over age 75?

_____

_____

_____

Name _____

# IT'S A WONDER!

**SECURITY FORCE NEEDED:** Your agency has been hired to provide security for a worldwide "Celebration of the Seven Natural Wonders of the World." Since you will need to make your own travel arrangements to visit each site, you must determine the geographic location of each and the approximate distance you will have to travel from your home to view each of the seven places.

List the seven wonders of the natural world and their locations in the order (nearest to farthest) that they are located in distance from your city or town. Place a star on the world map below to show each stop on your journey.

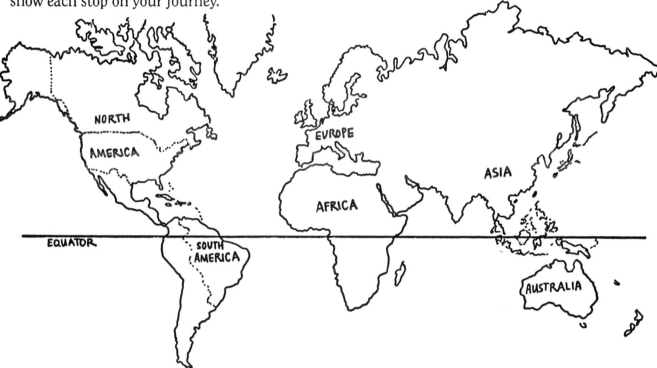

## THE SEVEN WONDERS OF THE NATURAL WORLD
### NAME                                    LOCATION

1. _____    _____
2. _____    _____
3. _____    _____
4. _____    _____
5. _____    _____
6. _____    _____
7. _____    _____

Note: Resources may disagree on which natural wonders are most significant. Choose any seven of those mentioned in your source.

Name _____

# SPORTS SLEUTHING

Your challenge is to see how quickly and accurately you can find information clues in a world almanac. Locate the answers requested here. Check the box at the bottom of the page that you think best categorizes your skills.

1. What man won the 1992 Olympic Figure Skating Gold Medal?

2. What horse was the Triple Crown winner of thoroughbred racing in 1977?

3. Who was the heavyweight boxing champion of the world from 1952-1956?

4. What is the only country to have won the World Cup Soccer championship four times?

5. What team won the World Series in baseball in the year you were born?

6. What woman won the tennis singles at Wimbledon, England for six consecutive years?

7. For what major sport were each of these names well known?

    Sonja Henie _____

    Boris Becker_____

    Micky Mantle _____

    Olga Korbut _____

    Joe Namath _____

    Jackie Joyner-Kersee _____

8. Who was awarded the Heisman Trophy as outstanding college football player in 1968?

9. What country dominated the Summer Olympic Championship in pole vaulting from 1896-1968?

10. What area of sports does each of these American sports organizations represent?

    NASCAR _____

    NRS _____

    PGA _____

    NFL _____

    NBA _____

    NHL _____

According to my score, I am a
    ☐ WINNER    ☐ CHAMPION    ☐ SUPER SLEUTH

Name _____

# UNCOMMON BUT COMMON

What do a nineteenth-century Quaker woman, a Mexican-American migrant worker, a Hawaiian senator, an African American congresswoman and the cofounder of *MS.* magazine have in common? Use your detecting skills to figure it out!

Use a biographical dictionary or encyclopedia to learn as much as possible about the lives and achievements of these five people. Record your findings briefly in the spaces below. Then decide what you believe is their common achievement.

|  | SUSAN BROWNELL ANTHONY | CESAR CHAVEZ | HIRAM FONG | SHIRLEY CHISHOLM | GLORIA ANTHONY STEINEM |
|---|---|---|---|---|---|
| *Dates:* | | | | | |
| *Home:* | | | | | |
| *Job(s):* | | | | | |

*Major Life Achievements*

SUSAN BROWNELL ANTHONY _____

_____

CESAR CHAVEZ _____

_____

HIRAM FONG _____

_____

SHIRLEY CHISHOLM _____

_____

GLORIA ANTHONY STEINEM _____

_____

## COMMON CONTRIBUTION TO SOCIETY

_____

_____

_____

Name _____

# WHO'S WHOSE SLEUTH?

The word *sleuth* came from a shortened form of *sleuth hound*, a Scottish bloodhound, noted for its perseverance in tracking game, suspects, or fugitives.

Below is a list of super sleuths of fiction who were, of course, named by their creators. Your mission is to draw a line to match the name of each sleuth with his or her creator. You will find encyclopedias or literary and biographical dictionaries to be helpful resources.

(A) Mickey Spillane

(B) Agatha Christie

(C) Rex Stout

(D) P. D. James

(E) G. K. Chesterton

(F) Earl Derr Biggers

(G) Leslie Charteris

(H) Agatha Christie

(I) John D. McDonald

(J) Erle Stanley Gardner

Charlie Chan
The Saint – Simon Templar
PERRY MASON
Miss Jane Marple
Father Brown
MIKE HAMMER
Hercule Poirot
Nero Wolfe
CORDELIA GRAY
Travis McGee

Name

# ONE FOR THE RECORD

For five decades, one of the world's best research groups has been the staff of Guinness Publishing Ltd. of Enfield, Great Britain. Each year, they publish a book of information that tells about the biggest and best in all kinds of categories.

I. Spend some time rummaging through the facts and figures in a recent *The Guinness Book of World Records.* In each space below, write an important record that interests you. Each entry must fit the word at the beginning of the line, and your final collection must include facts from at least eight different subject categories (e.g., all examples cannot be sports).

1. Oldest: _____

2. Biggest: _____

3. Smallest: _____

4. Fastest: _____

5. Longest: _____

6. Highest: _____

7. Lowest: _____

8. Greatest: _____

9. Youngest: _____

10. Deepest: _____

11. Worst: _____

12. Heaviest: _____

13. Lightest: _____

14. Most Valuable: _____

15. Strongest: _____

II. Check the name index in your record book to see if you can locate a person who shares either your first or last name.

Record the name here: _____

Tell what achievement is attributed to this person: _____

_____

_____

_____

Name _____

31

# THE BIG NEWS

You and your parents may think that the big news on the day of your birth was your arrival on the planet, but the newspaper headlines probably missed that very important story and chose something else instead. Sleuth on yourself. Visit your town library or your local newspaper office and see if you can find some of the following information.

On the day you were born:

1.  What was the front-page headline?

    _____

    _____

2.  What was the weather like? _____

    _____

3.  How much did the paper cost? _____

    _____

4.  What sporting event was making news? _____

    _____

5.  What politicians or world leaders were in the news? _____

    _____

6.  What were the popular cartoons? _____

    _____

7.  What movies were playing? _____

    _____

8.  Copy the headline of an article that tells some bad (unhappy) news. _____

    _____

9.  What was the "in" style in teen fashions? (See department store ads.) _____

    _____

10. What is the range of prices on a new pickup truck? _____

    _____

11. Name someone who died that week. _____

    _____

12. In this space, copy the most interesting "want ad" from the paper. _____

    _____

Name _____

# A BRILLIANT BIBLIOGRAPHY

One of a researcher's favorite words is *bibliography*—because in a bibliography, one can find gobs and gobs of information that is not in the usual reference books. Look up *bibliography* in your encyclopedia. Then use a grammar and composition textbook to review how bibliographies are written. You may find one that you can use as a model.

Choose one of the following topics and create a bibliography of at least ten resources that provide information on that topic. *Hint: Be sure to check the* Reader's Guide to Periodicals *for periodical items as well as a card catalog and any bibliographic information following encyclopedia entries.*

| | | |
|---|---|---|
| Prisoners of London Tower | Volcanoes | Famous Forgeries |
| Unsolved Mysteries | Outlaws of the Old West | Leprechauns |
| Magic & Magicians | Castles | Indian Legends |

Brilliant Bibliography Written On _____

1. _____

2. _____

3. _____

4. _____

5. _____

6. _____

7. _____

8. _____

9. _____

10. _____

Name _____

# QUICK? OR QUICKER?

As a researcher, you need to know which resource or reference gives you the fastest access to the information you need. Which of the following would be your first choice for locating the answer to each question below as quickly as possible?

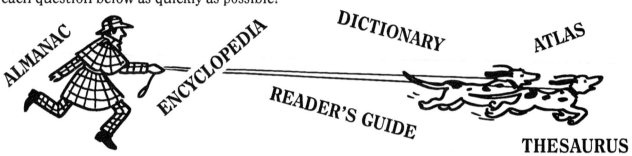

ALMANAC    ENCYCLOPEDIA    DICTIONARY    ATLAS    READER'S GUIDE    THESAURUS

Find each answer and note your "quickest" source.

1. What does a chronometer measure? _____
   Source: _____

2. What would you do with a foxglove? _____
   Source: _____

3. What's new in Chicago this year? _____
   Source: _____

4. According to a recent census, what is the population of the capital city in your state or province? _____ Source: _____

5. How is the word *animadversion* pronounced? _____
   Source: _____

6. In what year was Robert DeNiro born? _____
   Source: _____

7. What force causes a black hole in space? _____
   Source: _____

8. What is the approximate driving time from Chicago to San Francisco? _____
   Source: _____

9. What magazine recently published an article about vitamins? _____
   Source: _____

10. What are four good synonyms for the word *excellent*? _____
    Source: _____

11. Who won the Nobel Peace Prize in 1979? _____
    Source: _____

12. Which country is nearest the equator—Guatemala or Ecuador? _____
    Source: _____

Name _____

# KIDNAPPED!

A famous entertainer of the mid 1900s was kidnapped from his or her New York hotel room. Your job is to find out who the entertainer was; exactly when, where, and why he or she was kidnapped; and where he or she was held in captivity until his or her release. Use the clues below to track your case.

CLUE #1 The entertainer's first name is also the name of a U.S. state which is bordered by Georgia and six other states.

CLUE #2 The victim's middle name was shared by the famous American author who wrote A Farewell to Arms; however, it had been shortened to a nickname.

CLUE #3 The last name of the kidnapped person was the same as the last name of the famous industrialist who built a "Model T" automobile.

CLUE #4 He was abducted from a Manhattan hotel by the same name as a small Georgia town, located about 20 miles east of Dothan, Alabama, near the Chattahoochee River. The hotel also shares the first word in the name of one of the southern-most islands off the coast of South Carolina.

CLUE #5 The date of the kidnapping was the same month as the month in which the U.S. celebrates Veterans' Day. The day of the month was the same number as the longitude of Southport, England, and the year was the year that U.S. astronaut Neil Armstrong first set foot on the moon.

CLUE #6 He or she was held captive on an island located at latitude 58° S and longitude 27° W. (The island's name includes the name of an item commonly found on luncheon menus.)

CLUE #7 He or she was released when it was determined that he or she was a victim of mistaken identity. He or she was thought to be a playwright who won the Pulitzer Prize for drama in 1955 and was wanted for putting a cat on a hot tin roof.

---

## TRACK YOUR CLUES:

Entertainer by the name of #1 _____ #2 _____ #3 _____

was abducted from the #4 _____ Hotel in New York on the #5 _____ day

of #5 _____, #5_____. He or she (circle one) was held captive on #6 _____

Island, off the east coast of the #6 _____ continent, and was released when it was

discovered that because of a similarity in their names, he or she (circle one) had been confused

with playwright #7 _____ .

---

Name

# SLEUTHING TOOLS

If you're going to be a good sleuth, you have to know when and how to use which tools and techniques to gather information and prove the facts of your case. Some tools are more efficient than others for a given task. Circle the BEST FIRST source to check in each of the following cases.

1. You're trying to describe an "off-the-wall" teacher, and you're looking for some unusual adjectives.  dictionary  index
   thesaurus  biographical dictionary

2. You're writing a report about Olympic records.
   card catalog  almanac
   *The Guinness Book of World Records*  encyclopedia

3. You need to know the exact latitude and longitude of a South Pacific island.
   almanac  encyclopedia
   atlas  geographical dictionary

4. A research paper you are writing requires the statistics on population growth in major U.S. cities last year.
   encyclopedia  atlas
   encyclopedia index  almanac

5. You're curious to know the world record for the most sets of twins born to one family.
   encyclopedia index  *The Guinness Book of World Records*
   almanac  biographical dictionary

6. You want to make a replica of your state flag.
   atlas  encyclopedia
   card catalog  almanac

7. You need to make a list of the world's seven continents and note the bodies of water surrounding each.  encyclopedia  atlas
   almanac  geographical dictionary

8. You can't remember how to pronounce the word *dichotomy*.
   biology text glossary  thesaurus
   dictionary  language text glossary

9. You are researching to find the name most commonly used for a U.S. city.
   almanac  atlas index
   geographical dictionary  encyclopedia

10. On your essay about art appreciation, your teacher has commented on the over-use of the word *beautiful*. You need to edit!
    almanac  dictionary
    thesaurus  language text glossary

11. You're trying to locate the section in your language text that discusses subject-verb agreement.  text's table of contents  text's glossary
    text's index  text's preface

12. You are confused about whether to use the word *affect* or *effect* in a sentence.
    thesaurus  dictionary
    language text glossary  language text table of contents

Name

# FAST FIGURES

Your detective agency is located in a major city, but you must have quick access to other major cities if you are to be useful in solving crimes. How fast can you get to the scene? Below is a portion of the mileage chart located on your office wall. See if you can answer the following questions in record time. Get a friend to time you. Then invite your friend to do the same page and time him or her. Write your times at the bottom of the page. Which person would likely make the speediest reservations to get to the crime scene?

1. Of the following, which pair of cities is closer together? _____
   Albany, New York and Birmingham, Alabama or Boston, Massachusetts and Chicago, Illinois

2. What is the distance between Cleveland, Ohio and Boise, Idaho? _____

3. Is Boise, Idaho closer to Atlanta, Georgia or closer to Cheyenne, Wyoming? _____

4. How far is it from Charleston, South Carolina to Charleston, West Virginia? _____

5. If you live in Billings, Montana, would you travel farther
   to a Boston Red Sox or Atlanta Braves home game? _____

6. Of the cities listed on this chart, which is closest to Buffalo, New York? _____

7. Of the cities listed on this chart, which is the farthest from Baltimore, Maryland? _____

8. How many miles would you travel if you made a round trip
   between Albuquerque, New Mexico and Charlotte, North Carolina? _____

9. What two cities on this chart are farthest apart? _____

10. Approximately how many miles would you travel if you made
    a trip from Boston to Atlanta to Chicago and back to Boston? _____

|  | Albany NY | Albuquerque NM | Atlanta GA | Baltimore MD | Billings MT | Birmingham AL | Boise ID | Boston MA | Buffalo NY | Charleston SC | Charleston WV | Charlotte NC | Cheyenne WY | Chicago IL | Cleveland OH |
|---|---|---|---|---|---|---|---|---|---|---|---|---|---|---|---|
| Arcadia N.P. ME | 440 | 2459 | 1330 | 666 | 2468 | 1508 | 2958 | 274 | 733 | 1219 | 1039 | 1114 | 2221 | 1251 | 868 |
| Albany NY |  | 2041 | 1010 | 339 | 2098 | 1071 | 2518 | 169 | 301 | 880 | 636 | 772 | 1790 | 816 | 484 |
| Albuquerque NM | 2041 |  | 1404 | 1890 | 991 | 1254 | 940 | 2220 | 1773 | 1703 | 1600 | 1625 | 538 | 1312 | 1585 |
| Atlanta GA | 1010 | 1404 |  | 654 | 1799 | 150 | 2223 | 1108 | 907 | 291 | 501 | 240 | 1482 | 708 | 728 |
| Baltimore MD | 339 | 1890 | 654 |  | 1916 | 771 | 2406 | 427 | 365 | 568 | 362 | 418 | 1669 | 717 | 358 |
| Big Bend N.P. TX | 2239 | 586 | 1341 | 1907 | 1421 | 1192 | 1702 | 2297 | 1923 | 1623 | 1590 | 1583 | 966 | 1542 | 1732 |
| Billings MT | 2098 | 991 | 1799 | 1916 |  | 1775 | 606 | 2197 | 1721 | 2175 | 1721 | 1996 | 455 | 1231 | 1607 |
| Birmingham AL | 1071 | 1254 | 150 | 771 | 1775 |  | 2065 | 1226 | 902 | 441 | 561 | 391 | 1418 | 657 | 732 |
| Boise ID | 2518 | 940 | 2223 | 2406 | 606 | 2065 |  | 2685 | 2214 | 2493 | 2138 | 2345 | 734 | 1711 | 2026 |
| Boston MA | 169 | 2220 | 1108 | 427 | 2197 | 1226 | 2685 |  | 465 | 936 | 751 | 848 | 1923 | 1004 | 657 |
| Buffalo NY | 301 | 1773 | 907 | 365 | 1755 | 902 | 2214 | 465 |  | 925 | 446 | 707 | 1498 | 539 | 191 |
| Charleston SC | 880 | 1703 | 291 | 568 | 2175 | 441 | 2493 | 936 | 925 |  | 478 | 210 | 1710 | 906 | 726 |
| Charleston WV | 636 | 1600 | 501 | 362 | 1721 | 561 | 2138 | 751 | 446 | 478 |  | 268 | 1405 | 470 | 248 |
| Charlotte NC | 772 | 1625 | 240 | 418 | 1996 | 391 | 2345 | 848 | 707 | 210 | 268 |  | 1615 | 737 | 516 |
| Cheyenne WY | 1790 | 538 | 1482 | 1669 | 455 | 1418 | 734 | 1923 | 1498 | 1710 | 1405 | 1615 |  | 981 | 1326 |
| Chicago IL | 816 | 1312 | 708 | 717 | 1231 | 657 | 1711 | 1004 | 539 | 906 | 470 | 737 | 981 |  | 348 |
| Cleveland OH | 484 | 1585 | 728 | 358 | 1607 | 732 | 2026 | 657 | 191 | 726 | 248 | 516 | 1326 | 348 |  |
| Crater Lake N.P. OR | 2926 | 1357 | 2632 | 2800 | 1023 | 2470 | 417 | 3099 | 2633 | 2856 | 2514 | 2744 | 1151 | 2111 | 2442 |

RECORDED TIME: Player I _____ Player II _____

Name _____

# AT THE CRIME SCENE

Temperatures are often important pieces of evidence at crime scenes. You have been assigned as a partner to a pathologist who knows a lot about the qualities of blood at different temperatures. This partner needs to know what the temperature was at the crime scene for several hours. When she compares this information to blood found at the scene, it may help her to pin down the time of the crime. Your job is to chart and graph the temperature for each hour of the night up to the time the crime was discovered.

I. First, practice your graph reading skills so that you'll be ready to make your own graph.

1. What was the temperature at 10 P.M.?

2. At what time was the temperature below freezing?

3. At what two hours was the temperature the same?

4. Was the temperature lower at 1 A.M. or 11 P.M.?

5. At what time was the temperature 10 degrees higher than at 11 P.M.?

6. At what time was the temperature 45 degrees?

7. What was the lowest temperature before midnight?

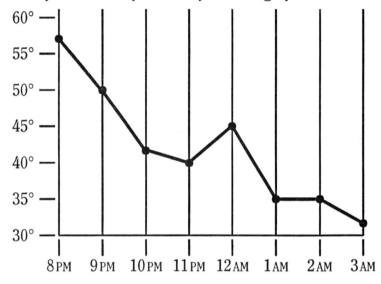

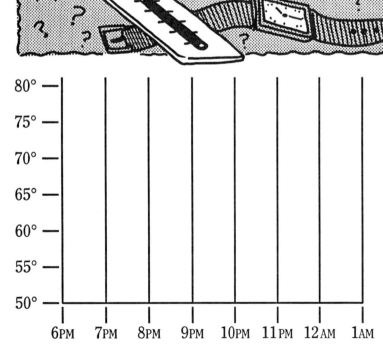

II. Graph the information about the temperatures on the night of this crime. Use the graph on the left:

• At 6 P.M. the temperature was 75°.
• At 7 P.M. the temperature was 71°.
• At 8 P.M. the temperature was 60°.
• At 9 P.M. the temperature was 60°.
• At 10 P.M. the temperature was 55°.
• At 11 P.M. the temperature was 53°.
• At 12 A.M. the temperature was 50°.

Name

# A DEADLY DIAGRAM

How good are you at reading diagrams? As a detective, you may be called upon at any time to read a diagram that demonstrates the exact location of a very important piece of evidence—such as a dead body!

Using the diagram below as your reference, see how quickly you can answer the following questions. Ask someone to time you. Then ask a friend to answer the same questions as you time him or her. Which of you is faster?

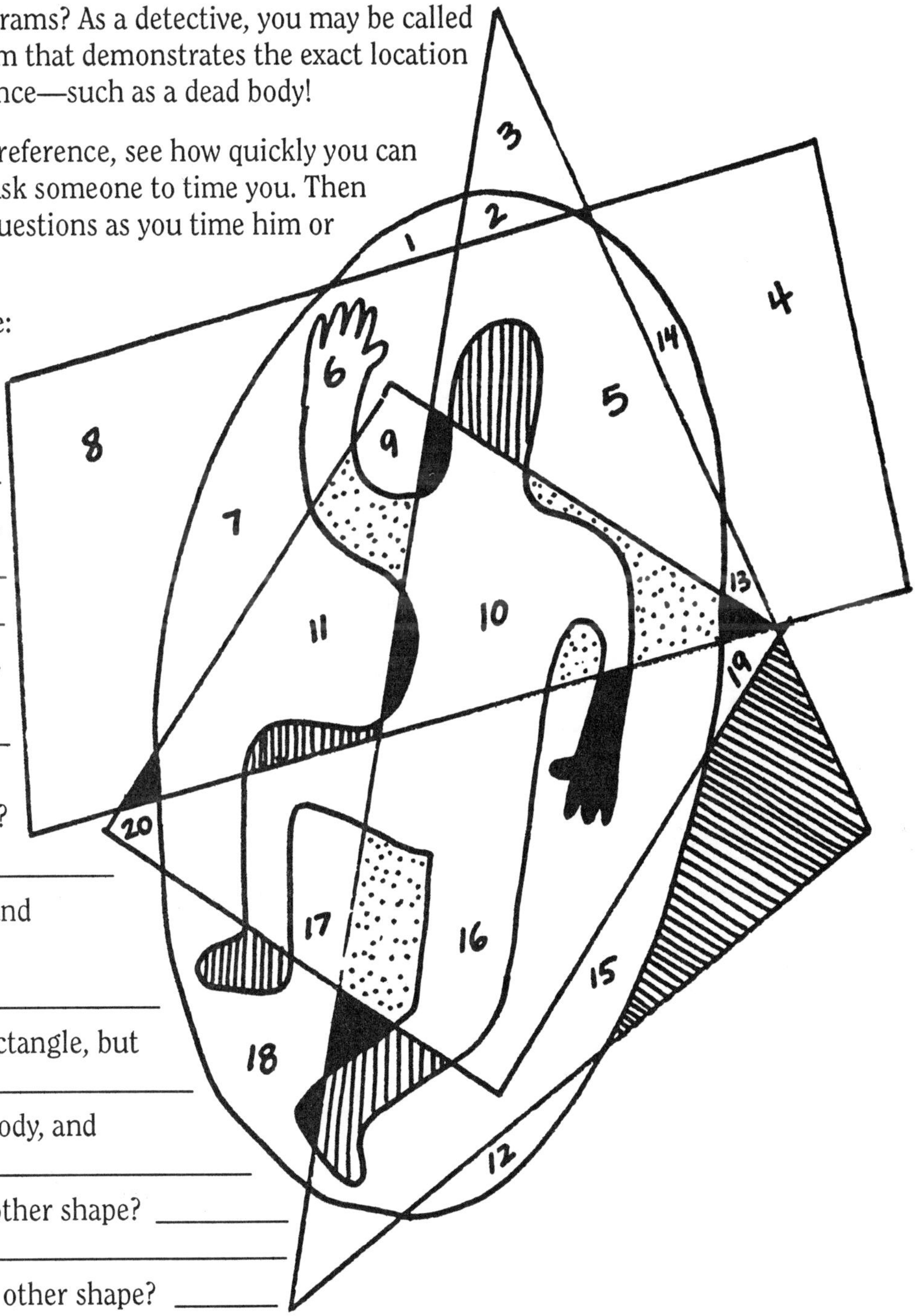

What numbers in the diagram are:

1. In both the triangle and rectangle, but not in the square or oval? _____ _____

2. Not in the body? _____ _____

3. In both the oval and rectangle, but not in the square or triangle? _____

4. In the rectangle, oval, and square, but not in the triangle? _____

5. In the square, triangle, body, and oval, but not in the rectangle? _____

6. In the triangle, square, and rectangle, but not in the oval? _____

7. In the triangle, square, oval, body, and rectangle? _____

8. In the square, but not in any other shape? _____ _____

9. In the triangle, but not in any other shape? _____ _____

10. In the body, but not in any other shape? _____

11. In the triangle, but not in the oval? _____

12. In the body, but not in the square? _____

Name _____

Basic Skills/Study & Research 6-8+

# NOSING AROUND IN HISTORY

| 3500 | Nile Civilization |
|------|-------------------|
| 3000 | Sumerians write in cuneiform |
|      | _____ 365-day calendar invented |
| 2500 | Egyptian Pyramids |
|      | Libraries open in Egypt<br>Indus River Civilization<br>Egyptian mummies made |
| 2000 | Percussion instruments added to Egyptian orchestra |
|      | _____ Code of Hammurabi |
| 1500 | Use of Iron; Egypt at height of glory |
|      | _____ Jewish exodus from Egypt<br>_____ Ten Commandments given to Moses |
| 1000 | King David rules Israel |
|      | _____ First coins minted |
| 500  | Birth of Buddha |
| B.C. | _____ Nebuchadnezzar II<br>_____ Alexander the Great<br>_____ Old Testament assembled |
| 0    | Birth of Christ |
| A.D. | |

Archeologists and historians are kinds of sleuths who dig way back into ancient history to "nose out" facts. The timeline on the left shows some of the facts they have been able to gather through various means. Study the timeline carefully. Then see if you can answer the questions that follow.

1. Number the order in which these periods of history occured:
   _____ The rule of Alexander the Great
   _____ The beginning of civilization along the Nile
   _____ The time of the kingdom of Israel

2. Which leader lived first?
   Buddha
   Alexander the Great
   Hammurabi
   King David

3. What event took place about 2000 years before the birth of Christ?

4. How many years elapsed between the invention of the 365-day calendar and the first minted coins?

5. How many years passed between the use of cuneiform writing and the first use of iron?

6. At about what time did Nebuchadnezzar II rule the Babylonian Empire?

7. If he had lived long enough, how old would Buddha have been when Christ was born?

8. What event occurred about the year 2750 B.C. that affects every day of our twentieth-century lives?

Name

# WANTED!

A group of notorious criminals who have changed their names and locations many times were recently caught and extradited to their native city of Washington, D.C. By observing closely the words and pictures of the news story below, see if you can identify the real name of each criminal and tell in what state, city, or country he was hiding. *(Hint: the names of the four criminals as well as the names of the places where they were hiding are hidden in the text of the story.)* If you are clever, you can match the names and places with the correct pictures. Underline them in the story and then fill in the blanks under the pictures.

---

**EX.**   The horse was rid**den ver**y hard down the river road and across Brevar**d Ave.** toward the river. (**Dave** was hiding in **Denver**.)

---

WASHINGTON (AP) Four of the FBI's top–ten wanted criminals were being extradited today from their various hideouts to face charges here in their home town. The clever sting operation which brought all four to Washington's Dulles airport within a four-hour period was initiated by a tip from ex-iconoscope operator Ted Mack, who observed one of the suspects trying to trade his pet cockatoo for land or a free lift ticket.

Fancy hats in a color adored by the second suspect, whose obsession is covering up his baldness, caused him to be trapped at a Florida beach-hut haberdashery.

A third fugitive, a former country singer, fell prey to the schemes of a female double agent— very chic, a gourmet dinner, . . .

The fourth man, known to have poor eyesight, had a minor accident on the plane which damaged his glasses; he literally fell into the hands of agents as he came through customs.

The successful search yesterday left the nefarious four few alternatives but to submit to arrest. They will appear in court on Tuesday.

Name _____

# EYEWITNESS REPORT

Something terrible has happened. Handsome Harry, on his way home from the library, was crushed by a load of bowling balls. The authorities found a scrap of paper clutched in his right hand—the last sentence of the novel *Moby Dick* by Herman Melville.

The scene looks like a tragic accident—but is it? You are the first detective at the scene. What questions will you ask the eyewitnesses? Will the clues lead you to the answer?

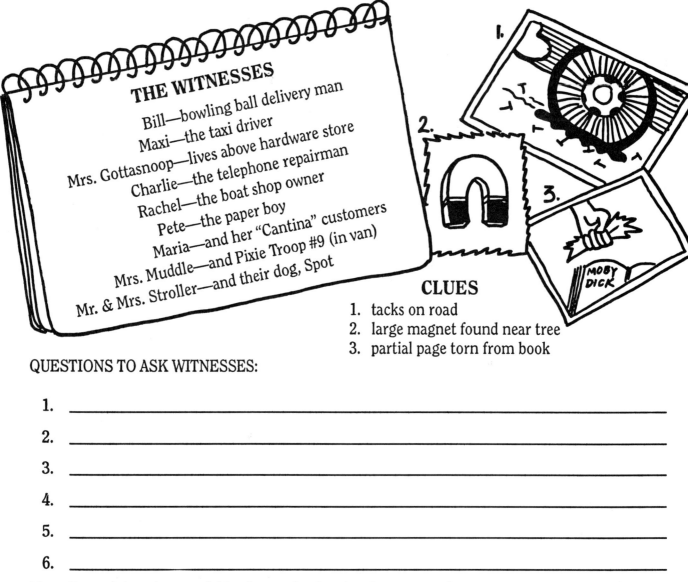

## THE WITNESSES

Bill—bowling ball delivery man
Maxi—the taxi driver
Mrs. Gottasnoop—lives above hardware store
Charlie—the telephone repairman
Rachel—the boat shop owner
Pete—the paper boy
Maria—and her "Cantina" customers
Mrs. Muddle—and Pixie Troop #9 (in van)
Mr. & Mrs. Stroller—and their dog, Spot

## CLUES

1. tacks on road
2. large magnet found near tree
3. partial page torn from book

QUESTIONS TO ASK WITNESSES:

1. _____

2. _____

3. _____

4. _____

5. _____

6. _____

Note: You might ask several friends to role-play the observers and answer your questions. Then come up with an hypothesis about what happened at the scene. You might then write a news story or a mystery show about the accident.

Use with page 43.

Name _____

Use with page 42.

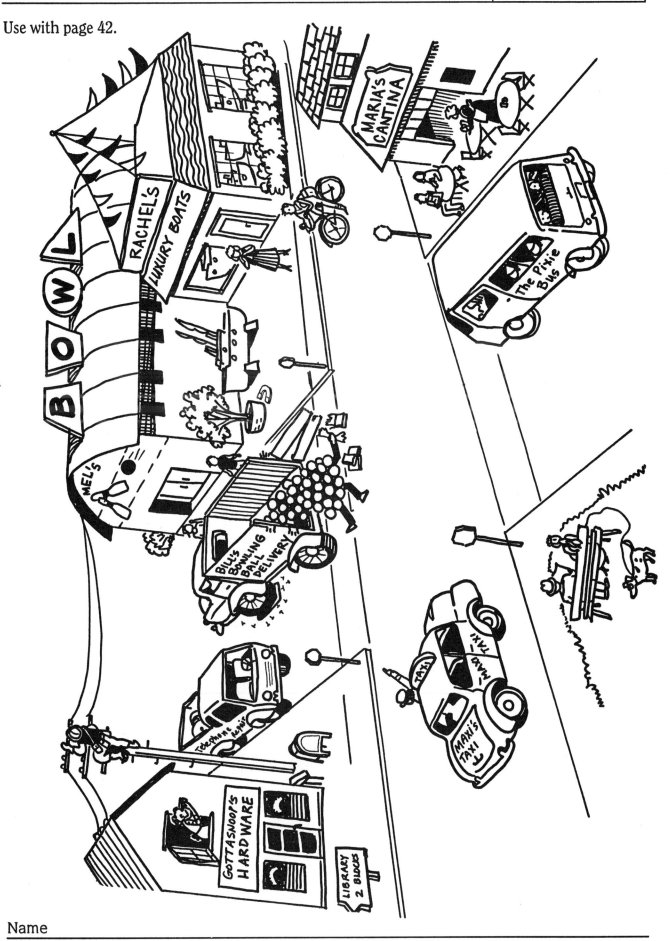

EYEWITNESS REPORT, CONTINUED

Name

# VOICES FROM THE PAST

"HIMSELF"
RED MAROON
b. 620
d. 695
A.D

Snooping for information and clues can take a detective to many places—maybe even to the cemetery. You'd be surprised at what you can learn about people, families, or even a whole community from a visit to the town cemetery.

Your job is to gather information about the people who lived in the past in the town where this cemetery is located (see page 45). Use these questions to help you gather some information from the cemetery. Write your answers here or on another piece of paper. Then organize the information to prepare a report about this community.

1. How many died before the age of 75?

2. How many died as children (16 or younger)?

3. How many gravestones have symbols, phrases, or epitaphs that are religious?

4. What kind of messages are found in the symbols or designs on the gravestones?

5. What clues do you find on the stones that let you know how some of these people wanted to be remembered?

6. What can you conclude about the Jackson family?

7. In what percentage of the family plots did the wife die before the husband?

8. What general statements about the community can you make from this picture?

9. Which gravestones do you find most interesting, and why?

10. By observing the general setting and appearance of the cemetery, can you make a generalization about the attitude of people in this community toward the care of their relatives after death?

Use with page 45.

Name

Use with page 44.

# CHANTICLEER AND THE FOX

**C**hanticleer was a clever but self-centered, conceited character whose chauvinistic attitude and foolish actions nearly resulted in great tragedy. He believed that he was, without question, the most gorgeous creature in the barnyard, and he strutted so proudly and crowed so loudly that no one would have dared to challenge him. In spite of his arrogance, his wives, the hens of the yard, rose early to preen and comb and prepare themselves to be chased by the most available and best looking husband in the feathered community. This chasing he did for his own pleasure and seemed not to notice if he scattered dust into the eyes of his wives or caused jealousies among them.

However, one young hen named Pertelote—the one most often favored by Chanticleer—was not entirely mesmerized by Chanticleer's charms. She recognized his arrogance and often reprimanded him for strutting too close to the edge of the forest where a sly fox lay in wait for a chance to de-feather a tasty meal.

"Who does he think he is?" retorted Chanticleer. "I am far too clever to be made into a mere snack for that silly fox!" But Pertelote continued to warn him, and he continued to ignore her. "I am more handsome than he, and my father has taught me to sing more beautifully than any forest animal. The fox is a second-class citizen!"

Then one day, as the hens were napping and Chanticleer sat preening on the fence near the forest, the sly fox saw his chance.

He sneaked to the fence, cocked his head, and whispered in his sly voice, "Good day, Chanticleer!"

Chanticleer nearly fell off the fence in fright, but the fox hastened to assure him that he had come with no ill intentions.

"I came only to ask of you a favor, " he lied. "I have fond memories of the beautiful songs of your father, and I have heard some of those same glorious sounds in recent days. I only beg you to throw your head back and close your eyes tight as your father once did, and sing to me. I am made lame by your tender music."

So filled with his prideful arrogance that he could not detect the deceit in the fox, though he knew full well his reputation, he threw his head back and crowed his most glorious notes.

Immediately, the fox grabbed him by the throat and carted him off to the forest. The ruckus was heard in the farmhouse as well as in the barnyard, and when the farmer and his sons saw their beautiful rooster being towed away by the neck, they ran after him, pitchforks in hand.

Chanticleer recognized the fox's predicament and capitalized upon the situation.

"Oh, Sir Fox, " he croaked. "How embarrassingly low-class of you to run from those humans. They are not half as swift or skilled as you are, and now that you are safely in your forest domain, why not turn and scold them away? Are they not much more afraid of you than you are of them?"

The fox, as vain as the cock, could not resist showing his superiority. And when he opened his mouth to belittle the farmer, of course, Chanticleer escaped to the highest tree!

— (Paraphrased from Chaucer's *Canterbury Tales*)

Name

# EYES-WISE

How fast can you pick up important clues and facts? A good detective needs to be able to get a quick overview of the most important information. You can check your skill at this by skimming the story "Chanticleer and the Fox" (found on page 46) and answering some questions to see if you picked up the important facts of the story.

A good method for skimming a story is to place your finger under each line and draw it across the page as you read. In doing this, your finger "pulls your eyes" across each line as quickly as possible. Do not look for details. Do not dwell on unfamiliar words. Just keep reading quickly!

I. Use the method above to skim the story. Ask someone to time you. When you're finished, write your "skim time" at the bottom of the page. See how many questions you can answer correctly without looking back at the story.

## QUESTIONS

1. What kind of a character is Chanticleer? Recall some of the words that were used to describe him.

   _____

2. How did Chanticleer treat the women in his life? _____

3. Who is Pertelote? _____

4. How did the fox trick Chanticleer? _____

5. Who chased the fox? _____

6. How did Chanticleer outwit the fox? _____

7. Where did Chanticleer go after he escaped the fox? _____

8. Where was the fox's home territory? _____

II. Now, reread the story carefully. Have someone time you again. (Do not use your finger!) Write your reading time at the bottom of the page. Then use a pen or pencil of a different color to fill in any answers you could not answer after skimming.

Skim time _____

Read time _____

Name _____

# GET ORGANIZED!

In crime detection, as in any career, it is important to be able to organize information clearly so that other readers may have a precise understanding of the story. Practice your skills by organizing the main details of the story "Chanticleer and the Fox" into outline form for the purpose of exposing the character of Chanticleer. Your outline will help you write a precise report on what Chanticleer was like.

**I. Main Idea** (first outstanding characteristic)

_____

A. Subtopic (first supporting statement)

_____

   1.  Detail (first proof) _____

   2.  Detail (second proof) _____

B. Subtopic (second supporting statement)

_____

   1.  Detail (first proof) _____

   2.  Detail (second proof) _____

**II. Main Idea** (second outstanding characteristic)

_____

A. Subtopic (first supporting statement)

_____

   1.  Detail (first proof) _____

   2.  Detail (second proof) _____

B. Subtopic (second supporting statement)

_____

   1.  Detail (first proof) _____

   2.  Detail (second proof) _____

The above pattern may be continued to include a third or fourth idea if needed.

Name _____

# SUCCINCTLY SPEAKING

When you and a partner are working on a mystery case, each of you has to be able to give the other a quick run-down—a succinct summary—of the information you have gathered separately.

Practice doing this by summarizing as completely, but as concisely, as possible, the story of "Chanticleer and the Fox." Pretend you were sitting in a tree above the barnyard, observing the entire turn of events. What happened?

Write the abridged version here!

**CHANTICLEER AND THE FOX**
*A succinct summary*

BY: _____

Name
_____

# MEDIA-IN-A-MINUTE

Being able to quickly summarize a situation is a skill that is very advantageous to sleuthing. What's going on here? What does it mean? Practice your sleuthing summary skills by writing a brief but accurate summary of a TV program, a movie, and a book. Each of the three must be able to be read (by a good reader) in a minute! Then for each summary, identify the main thesis—the big idea or message—of each piece.

I. Summarize an episode from your favorite TV program.

_____

_____

_____

_____

What was the main thesis or message of this program? _____

_____

_____

II. Summarize one of your favorite movies.

_____

_____

_____

_____

Identify the main thesis or message intended for the viewers by the creators. _____

_____

_____

III. Summarize one of your favorite books.

_____

_____

_____

_____

What message or idea did the author intend for the reader? _____

_____

_____

Name _____

# FOLLOW THE NUMBERS

Every detective has a little black book of numbers. In the late 1800s, an American librarian named Melvil Dewey invented a system of numbers for keeping track of books—all the nonfiction books in a library. This numerical system divides all books into ten categories of knowledge, each of which has a specific set of numbers assigned to it.

Most school libraries are set up on the Dewey Decimal System. When a book is added to the collection, the librarian uses the Dewey Decimal system to assign it a "call number"—its own group of numbers within its classification category. This number is put on the spine of the book so it can be seen while the book is on the shelf. Since the numbers must follow the system guidelines, books about the same subject will always be found close to each other.

The chart below shows the ten groups and the numbers for each. Finish the third and fourth sections of the chart by finding books in your library that fit into each category. Write each title in its appropriate place. Then in the fourth section, write a simple phrase that tells what the books in each group are about.

| Dewey Numbers | Group Name | Book Title | Description |
|---|---|---|---|
| 000-099 | General Works | | |
| 100-199 | Philosophy | | |
| 200-299 | Religion | | |
| 300-399 | Social Studies | | |
| 400-499 | Language | | |
| 500-599 | Pure Science | | |
| 600-699 | Applied Science | | |
| 700-799 | Fine Arts | | |
| 800-899 | Literature | | |
| 900-999 | History, Geography, Biography | | |

Name _____

# FINGER-FAST INFORMATION

The card catalog was created for finding information fast. It's a detective's dream. You can locate any book in a library by searching the card catalog under its title, its author, or its subject.

On the list below, there are items missing in two of the three columns. Use a card catalog or on-line catalog in your library to locate the missing pieces. Fill in each empty space under "author," "book title," and "subject."

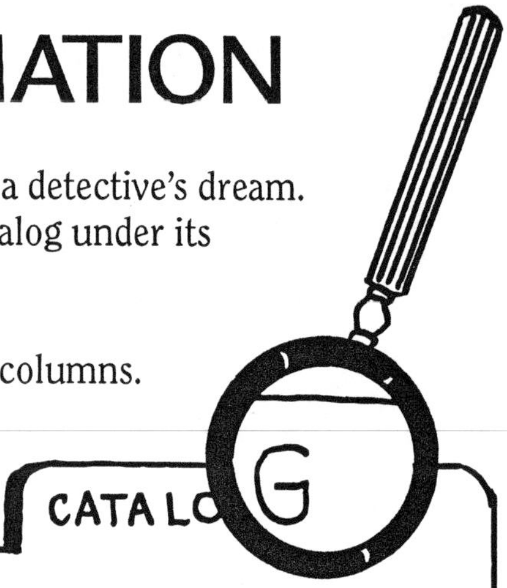

CATALOG

| | AUTHOR | BOOK TITLE | SUBJECT |
|---|---|---|---|
| 1. | | *Anne of Green Gables* | |
| 2. | Louisa May Alcott | | |
| 3. | | *The Illustrated Man* | |
| 4. | | *Huckleberry Finn* | |
| 5. | | | Scotland Yard |
| 6. | William Golding | | |
| 7. | | *Pride & Prejudice* | |
| 8. | | | Earthquakes |
| 9. | Arthur Conan Doyle | | |
| 10. | | | Daniel Boone |
| 11. | Jules Verne | | |
| 12. | Agatha Christie | | |
| 13. | | *Great Expectations* | |
| 14. | | | Mystery |
| 15. | C. S. Lewis | | |
| 16. | | *A Wrinkle in Time* | |
| 17. | | | Crime |
| 18. | | | Chemistry |

Name

# APPENDIX

## CONTENTS

# WHICH REFERENCE IS WHICH?

**Atlas:** A book of maps. Atlases give geographical information in the forms of maps, tables, graphs, and lists.

**Almanac:** A yearly publication that gives information on many topics. Almanacs are organized with an alphabetical index which lists information by categories.

**Bibliography:** Found at the end of many books or articles, this gives a list of the sources used in the publication.

**Biographical Dictionary:** Gives a brief résumé of a famous person's life and accomplishments. Entries are listed alphabetically.

**Card Catalog:** Contains three cards for every book in the library. These cards are filed separately. There is an author card, which is filed alphabetically by the author's last name; a subject card, which is filed alphabetically according to the subject of the book, and a title card, which is filed alphabetically according to the title of the book. In many libraries, card catalog information is now found on computers.

**Dictionary:** Lists the standard words of a particular language alphabetically and provides their meanings and pronunciation. Many dictionaries also provide other information about the word, such as part of speech, uses, antonyms, and etymologies.

**Encyclopedia:** A set of books providing information on many branches of knowledge. Usually there are many volumes. Information is arranged alphabetically according to the topic or name of person, place, or event.

**Encyclopedia Index:** A volume at the end of the encyclopedia which lists the subjects of the whole set alphabetically. It tells which volumes and pages hold information related to the subject.

**Encyclopedia Yearbook:** Published each year. This is an extra volume to an encyclopedia set, which gives information about current events of the past year.

**Gazetteer:** A geographical dictionary, listing information about important places in the world. Subjects and places are listed alphabetically.

**Geographical Dictionary:** The same as a gazetteer.

**The Guinness Book of World Records:** An annual collection of information of extraordinary facts and records

**Index:** Usually found at the end of a book, magazine, or other publication, it alphabetically lists information found in that volume.

**The Kane Book of Famous First Facts:** A listing of facts about firsts of many kinds, listed alphabetically.

**Magazine or Newspaper Index:** These list the subjects and titles of articles in a particular magazine or newspaper, or a particular group of magazines or newspapers.

**Quotation Indexes:** Listings of famous quotations and persons who said them (listed alphabetically by the first word of the quotation and by the last name of the persons).

**Special Encyclopedias:** A book or set of books that gives information on a particular field of knowledge, such as science, art, music, history, or sports.

**Table of Contents:** Gives an outline of the information contained in a book, listed in order that the information occurs in the book.

**Thesaurus:** A dictionary of synonyms. Words are listed in alphabetical order. Sometimes words are grouped according to topics.

55

# FINDING YOUR WAY AROUND THE LIBRARY

## THE DEWEY DECIMAL SYSTEM
*(Simplified)*

The ten major classes that make up the Dewey Decimal System of Classification are:

000-099 ...................... GENERAL WORKS

100-199 ................ IDEAS: PHILOSOPHY

200-299 .................................. RELIGION

300-399 .................... SOCIAL SCIENCES

400-499 ................................ LANGUAGE

500-599 ......................... PURE SCIENCE

600-699 .................. USES OF SCIENCE, TECHNOLOGY

700-799 ................................ FINE ARTS

800-899 ............................ LITERATURE

900-999 ................................... HISTORY, GEOGRAPHY, BIOGRAPHY

## LIBRARY OF CONGRESS SYSTEM
*(Simplified)*

The major classes that make up the Library of Congress System of Classification are:

A   GENERAL WORKS

B   PHILOSOPHY, RELIGION

C   SUBJECTS RELATED TO HISTORY

D   WORLD HISTORY

E-F   NORTH AMERICAN HISTORY
     SOUTH AMERICAN HISTORY

G   GEOGRAPHY, ANTHROPOLOGY

H   SOCIAL SCIENCES

J   LAW

K   POLITICS

L   EDUCATION

M   MUSIC

N   THE ARTS

P   LANGUAGE, LITERATURE

Q   SCIENCE

R   MEDICINE

S   AGRICULTURE

T   TECHNOLOGY

U   ARMIES

V   NAVIES

Z   BOOK LISTS, LIBRARIES

# STUDY & RESEARCH
# SKILLS TEST

Each question is worth 2 points. Total possible points is 100.

1. Put these words in alphabetical order:
   1. perform    _____
   2. prickly    _____
   3. pharaoh    _____
   4. pizza      _____
   5. panic      _____
   6. poorhouse  _____

2. Put these words in alphabetical order:
   1. mystery     _____
   2. mystify     _____
   3. mysterious  _____
   4. mystical    _____
   5. mysteries   _____
   6. mystic      _____
   7. mystique    _____
   8. mysticism   _____

3. Which of the following topics would fall on an encyclopedia page which has the guide words *BERMUDA TRIANGLE* and *BIGFOOT*? Circle those words that would.

   bicarbonate of soda     beta particle

   Bill of Rights     binoculars

   bighorn sheep     Bible

   biathlon     Berlin, Irving

   Bernhardt, Sarah     beeswax

   Better Business Bureau     bronchitis

4. Where would you look in a book to find when it was first printed?
   a. title page     b. table of contents
   c. index     d. copyright page

5. Where would you find a listing of the sections of the book?
   a. index     b. bibliography
   c. table of contents     d. glossary

Use the map below to answer 6–10.

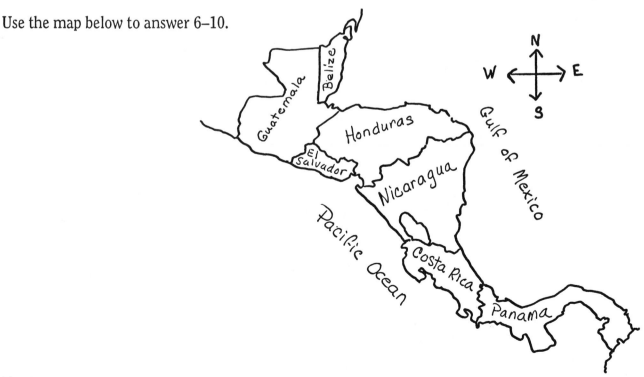

Name _____

6. How many countries border Guatemala on the south and east? _____

7. How many countries border both the Pacific Ocean and the Gulf of Mexico? _____

8. What country borders Guatemala but not Honduras? _____

9. Which of these Central American countries do not border the Gulf of Mexico?

   _____

10. Which countries extend farther east than Honduras? _____

   _____

Use the chart below to answer 11-15.

| MYSTERY CASE ASSIGNMENTS | | | | | | |
|---|---|---|---|---|---|---|
| **Case Type** | **# Cases Given to Detectives** | | | | | |
| | J. Jolly | S. Snoop | U. P. Tight | I. V. League | S. Wiley | B. Sharp |
| Robberies | 41 | 3 | 7 | 13 | 6 | 21 |
| Missing Persons | 7 | 4 | 9 | 2 | 6 | 11 |
| Missing Animals | 12 | 31 | 20 | 17 | 37 | 41 |
| Assaults | 6 | 12 | 16 | 22 | 19 | 11 |
| Car Thefts | 3 | 1 | 0 | 0 | 0 | 2 |
| Break-Ins | 4 | 0 | 17 | 6 | 22 | 18 |
| Suspicious Noises | 4 | 18 | 29 | 42 | 40 | 29 |

11. What kind of case did Detective Snoop investigate most frequently? _____

12. What kind of case was least common? _____

13. What kind of case was most common? _____

14. Which detective handled the most break-ins? _____

15. Which kind of case did Detective Jolly handle most frequently? _____

16. What kind of reference gives you synonyms for words? _____

17. What kind of reference supplies definitions and pronunciations of words? _____

18. What kind of reference contains a wide variety of facts that are up to date? _____

19. What kind of reference contains a lot of maps? _____

20. What kind of reference gives brief descriptions of important persons? _____

21. What kind of reference supplies histories of words? _____

22. What kind of reference supplies in-depth information about
    a wide variety of people, places, events, and other topics? _____

Name _____

Use the graph at the right to answer 23-26.

**Unsolved Cases**
J. J. Creep, P.I.

_____ 23. In what years did unsolved cases total over 50?

_____ 24. In how many years were there more cases closed than left open?

_____ 25. Between which two years was there the greatest drop in unsolved cases?

_____ 26. How many unsolved cases remained open in 1997?

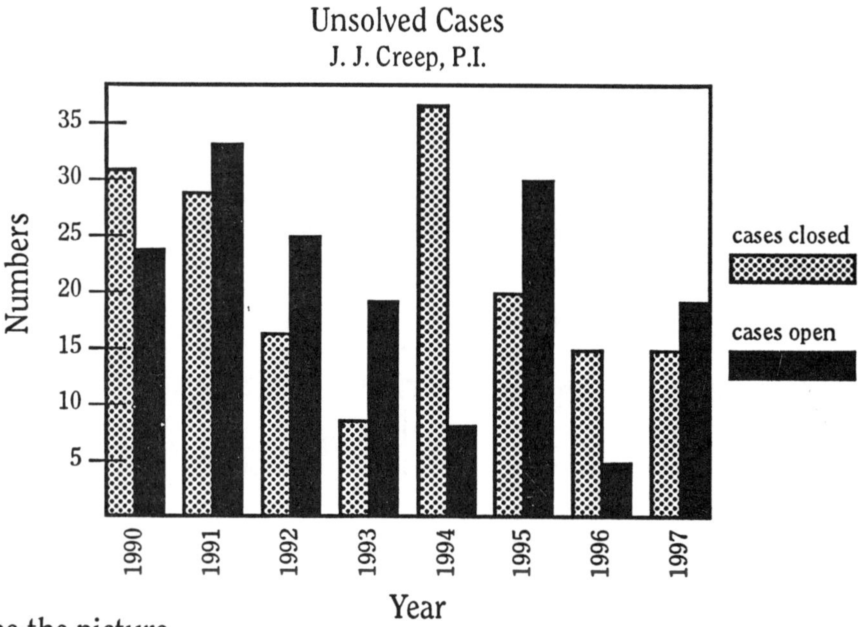

Use careful observation skills to examine the picture at the right. Describe four things you notice that give you information about clues to what has happened in this scene.

27. _____

_____

_____

28. _____

_____

_____

29. _____

_____

_____

30. _____

_____

_____

What word would you first look under in an encyclopedia to find each of the topics below? (31-34)

___ 31. President John Kennedy
    a. president     b. John
    c. Kennedy     d. government

___ 32. Temperatures in the English Channel
    a. weather     b. England
    c. English Channel     d. temperature

___ 33. Famous mystery radio programs
    a. radio     b. mystery
    c. detectives     d. programs

___ 34. Farthest planet from Earth?
    a. planets     b. Earth
    c. space     d. solar system

Name

   

Which reference book would be the best source in which to find each of these? (35-40)

___ 35. the best-selling mysteries of Agatha Christie
   a. almanac
   b. thesaurus
   c. *The Guinness Book of World Records*
   d. biographical dictionary

___ 36. the founder of the city of Chicago
   a. encyclopedia
   b. atlas
   c. dictionary
   d. card catalog

___ 37. the current population of California
   a. atlas
   b. almanac
   c. encyclopedia
   d. *The Kane Book of Famous First Facts*

___ 38. if it was Thomas Jefferson who said, "Give me liberty or give me death"
   a. special encyclopedia
   b. quotation index on history
   c. almanac
   d. gazetteer

___ 39. if *ambidextrous* is spelled correctly
   a. thesaurus
   b. index
   c. dictionary
   d. encyclopedia

___ 40. the first woman to climb Mt. Everest
   a. *The Guinness Book of World Records*
   b. *The Kane Book of Famous First Facts*
   c. atlas
   d. encyclopedia

In what section of the Dewey Decimal System would you find these? (41-45)

___ 41. A book of African poetry
   a. 200-299
   b. 800-899
   c. 400-499
   d. 300-399

___ 42. A biography of Walt Disney
   a. 000-099
   b. 500-599
   c. 900-999
   d. 600-699

___ 43. A book that has facts about shooting stars
   a. 500-599
   b. 700-799
   c. 400-499
   d. 200-299

___ 44. A book of puns
   a. 200-299
   b. 800-899
   c. 700-799
   d. 400-499

___ 45. A science encyclopedia
   a. 000-099
   b. 100-199
   c. 300-399
   d. 500-599

___ 46. What card in the card catalog would you search for to find a book on diseases?
   a. subject card   b. author card   c. title card

___ 47. What card in the card catalog would you look for to find a book of spooky poems by Edgar Allen Poe?
   a. subject card   b. author card   c. title card

___ 48. Which would you find in the *R* section of the Library of Congress classification system?
   a. a book of chemistry experiments
   b. a book about U.S. presidential elections
   c. a book describing different medicines
   d. a biography of a musician

___ 49. In which section of the Library of Congress system would you expect to find this book: *Black Holes and Wormholes: Mysteries of Deep Space?*
   a. Section D
   b. Section V
   c. Section H
   d. Section Q

___ 50. Which sentence best summarizes the paragraph below?
   a. Detectives need special training for their work.
   b. People hire detectives for some pretty strange jobs.
   c. Detectives have to work odd hours.
   d. A detective's job is dangerous.

*The day began with a call from a Mrs. Squeal who was looking for a detective who could find the kittens her cat had given birth to and deserted. Detective Smogg went from that case to investigate a man's claim that his next-door neighbor was putting poison in his vegetable garden. The next case was to follow the trail of a brother-in-law who had disappeared along with his wife's seven wigs. After lunch, the detective finished some paperwork on a case where a family suspected a hobo was sleeping in their garage, and located a box of lost pet crickets. By dark, he was ready to resume his nighttime stake-out to locate the howling dog that was constantly bothering the Nervy family. Just when he thought he could quit for the night, a 2 a.m. call came, asking him to figure out why Mrs. Ears was hearing repeated sneezing in her house all night, when there was no one there but herself.*

SCORE: Total Points _____ out of a possible 100 points

Name

# STUDY & RESEARCH
# SKILLS TEST ANSWER KEY

1.  1. panic
    2. perform
    3. pharaoh
    4. pizza
    5. poorhouse
    6. prickly
2.  1. mysteries
    2. mysterious
    3. mystery
    4. mystic
    5. mystical
    6. mysticism
    7. mystify
    8. mystique
3.  bicarbonate of soda
    beta particle
    Bible
    biathlon
    Bernhardt, Sarah
    Better Business Bureau
4.  d
5.  c
6.  3
7.  5
8.  Belize
9.  El Salvador
10. Nicaragua, Costa Rica, Panama
11. missing animals
12. car thefts
13. suspicious noises
14. Detective S. Wiley
15. robberies
16. thesaurus
17. dictionary
18. almanac
19. atlas
20. biographical dictionary

21. dictionary
22. encyclopedia
23. 1990, 1991, 1992, 1995
24. 3
25. 1994-96
26. 19
27–30. Answers will vary. Give credit for any insightful observations students make about the scene. (e.g. open safe, picture on floor, window broken, glass lying outside, weather, shape of footprints, lack of water inside, keys on floor, broken necklace, broken lamp, direction of footprints, etc.)
31. c
32. c
33. b
34. d
35. d
36. a
37. b
38. b
39. c
40. b
41. b
42. c
43. a
44. d
45. d
46. a
47. b
48. c
49. d
50. b

Basic Skills/Study & Research 6-8+

61

Copyright ©1997 by Incentive Publications, Inc., Nashville, TN.

# ANSWERS

**Page 10**

THE CHEF BAKED
IT IN A PIE

**Page 11**

| TOP: | BOTTOM: |
|------|---------|
| 1. G | 1. Zagreb |
| 2. F | 2. Zambezi |
| 3. P | 3. Zanzibar |
| 4. C | 4. Zapotec |
| 5. D | 5. Zedikiah |
| 6. E | 6. Zen |
| 7. M | 7. Zeppelin |
| 8. N | 8. Zeus |
| 9. J | 9. ziggurat |
| 10. L | 10. Zimbabwe |
| 11. A | 11. zinc |
| 12. Q | 12. zinnia |
| 13. T | 13. Zircon |
| 14. I | 14. zither |
| 15. R | 15. zodiac |
| 16. K | 16. zola |
| 17. S | 17. zoology |
| 18. B | 18. zoonosis |
| 19. O | 19. Zuider Zee |
| 20. H | 20. Zurich |

**Pages 12-13**

1. 33-37
2. 118-149
3. 150-175
4. 235
5. 190-194
6. 89-91
7. 16-31, 230

8. 43
9. 70-117
10. 140
11. 195–197
12. 100, 101, 123

**Pages 14-15**

1. 100
2. 41
3. 287, 114
4. 28, 175
5. 264
6. 194–196, 204–209, 210-223
7. 19
8. 90–109, 288–289, 292
9. 250–251, 256–259, 266, 272
10. 120–135, 191, 211
11. 21
12. 52–53
13. 192–193, 224
14. 25
15. 199
16. 13
17. 47, 192–193, 202–203, 222
18. 216, 217
19. 154–160
20. 189, 201

**Page 16**

(see below)

**Page 17**

maps will vary

**Page 18**

1. a right, granted by law, to a composer, author, or publisher to exclusive publication of a work

2. from the time it is created until 50 years after the author's death (75 years after creation if anonymous)

3. *Math in the Real World of Architecture* and *Brothers and Other Annoyances*

4. *Math in the Real World of Architecture*

5. Dr. I. Noahtall

6. *Training Your Pet Python, Brothers and Other Annoyances, Tales That Twist Your Tongue*

7. *Training Your Pet Python*

8. Bodyworks Press, Inc.

9. *Training Your Pet Python*

10. *Math in the Real World of Architecture*

**Page 19**

| | |
|------|-------|
| 1. Q | 14. B |
| 2. S | 15. I |
| 3. E | 16. F |
| 4. R | 17. L |
| 5. U | 18. M |
| 6. P | 19. T |
| 7. N | 20. C |
| 8. Y | 21. D |
| 9. O | 22. G |
| 10. J | 23. K |
| 11. X | 24. W |
| 12. H | 25. A |
| 13. V | |

**Page 20**

Answers will vary.

**Page 21**

1. Boston, Budapest, Birmingham, Boise
2. Answers will vary.
3. Brazzaville
4. Bogotá
5. Baffin Island
6. Brisbane
7. Bulgaria
8. Bhutan
9. Bratislava & Budapest
10. Beirut
11. Answers will vary.

**Page 22**

(see below)

---

**Page 16**

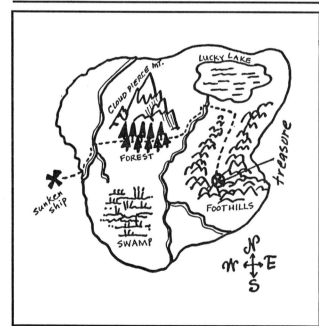

**Page 22**

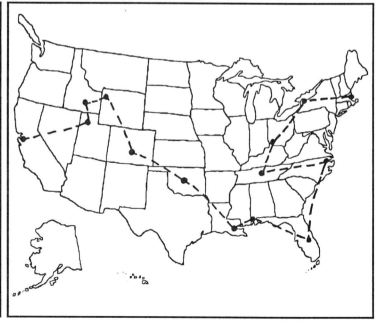

---

## Page 23

1. The brilliant detective in many of Agatha Christie's famous mysteries
2. A mystery of deep space— a hypothetical passageway in space and time
3. Volcanic island in the South Pacific that mysteriously appears and disappears
4. Well-known TV mystery-suspense series
5. Secret religious rites of ancient Greece
6. Also known as a "ghost" fish
7. Pilot who disappeared with her plane on an around-the-world flight in 1937—no trace was ever found.
8. The name of one of Agatha Christie's most famous mysteries, about a murder which takes place on the train "The Orient Express"
9. A fabled monster of Greek legend, with human head and a lion's body—legend is that the sphinx asked a mysterious riddle of anyone who passed it, and those who couldn't answer were killed.
10. Another of Agatha Christie's detectives—an old lady who solves crimes as a pastime
11. A lonely island west of Chile, with huge rock monoliths, the origin of which is a mystery
12. A mysterious disappearing ship
13. Detective main character of Mickey Spillane's mysteries
14. Playwright who wrote a famous play called "Ghosts"
15. A 1968 study of UFO sightings
16. An area in the Atlantic Ocean near Bermuda where about 70 ships and planes are said to have mysteriously disappeared leaving no trace
17. copies of old manuscripts of Biblical times, which were missing and searched for over centuries
18. American ship from which all passengers and crew mysteriously disappeared—a mystery never solved
19. 1952 U.S.Air Force Project to investigate the possibility of UFOs
20. French composer who created a piece of music called "The Mysterious Barricades"

## Page 24

| | |
|---|---|
| 1. c | 8. c and d |
| 2. c | 9. a |
| 3. b | 10. c |
| 4. c | 11. b |
| 5. d | 12. c |
| 6. d | 13. c |
| 7. a | 14. a |

## Page 25

Answers will vary due to differences in encyclopedia sets.

## Page 26

Answers will vary.

## Page 27

Answers may vary, as different sources list different "wonders." A possible set:
1. Mt. Everest — south central Asia
2. Victoria Falls — on Zambezi River in south central Africa
3. Grand Canyon —Arizona
4. Great Barrier Reef—Coral Sea, off east coast of Australia
5. Northern Lights—skies of the far northern hemispheres
6. Paricutin volcano —west of Mexico City
7. Harbor at Rio de Janeiro, Brazil— Brazil

## Page 28

1. Victor Petrenko
2. Seattle Slew
3. Rocky Marciano
4. Brazil
5. answers will vary
6. Martina Navratilova
7. Henie—figure skating
   Mantle—baseball
   Namath—football
   Becker—tennis
   Korbut—gymnastics
   Kersee—track & field
8. O. J. Simpson
9. United States
10. NASCAR—car racing
    NRS—shooting
    PGA—golf
    NFL—football
    NBA—basketball
    NHL—ice hockey

## Page 29

Susan Brownwell Anthony: 1820–1906, Rochester, NY, school teacher, crusader for women's right to vote

Cesar Chavez, 1927– , Arizona, Migrant Worker, started National Farm Workers Association, a labor union for Mexican-American migrant workers' families

Hiram Fong, 1925– , Hawaii, laborer & lawyer & senator, worked to unite races

Shirley Chisholm, 1924– , Brooklyn, NY, educator and first black congress-woman, worked for laws raising standard of living for poor of all races

Gloria Steinem, 1934– , NY, NY, writer & speaker & feminist, worked for equal rights for minority groups, especially women

## Page 30

F—Charlie Chan
G—The Saint-Simon Templar
J—Perry Mason
B or H—Miss Jane Marple
A—Mike Hammer
H or B—Hercule Perot
C—Nero Wolfe
E—Father Brown
D—Cordelia Gray
I—Travis McGee

## Page 31

Answers will vary.

## Page 32

Answers will vary.

## Page 33

Answers will vary.

## Page 34

1. precise time—dictionary
2. plant it or put it in a flower arrangement—dictionary
3. answers will vary—Reader's Guide
4. answers will vary— almanac
5. dictionary
6. 1943—almanac
7. gravity—encyclopedia
8. 45 hours or 2175 miles—atlas
9. answers will vary—Reader's Guide
10. answers will vary—thesaurus
11. Mother Theresa—almanac
12. Ecuador—atlas

## Page 35

1 Tennessee
2 Ernie
3 Ford
4 Hilton
5 3rd
5 November
5 1969
6 South Sandwich
7 Tennessee Williams

**Page 36**
1. thesaurus
2. almanac
3. atlas
4. almanac
5. *The Guinness Book*
6. encyclopedia
7. atlas
8. dictionary
9. atlas index
10. thesaurus
11. language text's index
12. dictionary

**Page 37**
1. Boston and Chicago
2. 2026 mi
3. Cheyenne
4. 478 mi
5. Boston Red Sox
6. Albany, NY
7. Boise, ID
8. 3250 mi
9. Boston, MA and Crater Lake, OR
10. approx. 2820 mi

**Page 38**
(see above right)

**Page 39**
1. 13
2. 1, 2, 3, 4, 5, 7, 8, 9, 11, 12, 13, 14, 15, 17, 18, 19, 20
3. 6, 7, 14
4. 9, 11
5. 16
6. 13
7. 10
8. 20
9. 3
10. none
11. 3, 13, 19
12. 6

**Page 40**
1. 3, 1, 2
2. Hammurabi
3. Egyptians added percussion instruments to the orchestra
4. 2000 years
5. 1500 years
6. about 400 B.C.
7. 500 years old
8. 365-day calendar was invented

**Page 41**
1. Walter, hiding in Mexico
2. Archy, hiding in Chicago
3. Adam, hiding in Orlando
4. Tom, hiding in Colorado

**Page 38**
I. 1. 41°
2. 3 A.M.
3. 1 A.M. and 2 A.M.
4. 1 A.M.
5. 9 P.M.
6. 9:30 P.M. and 12 A.M.
7. 40°

II. Graph should look like this:

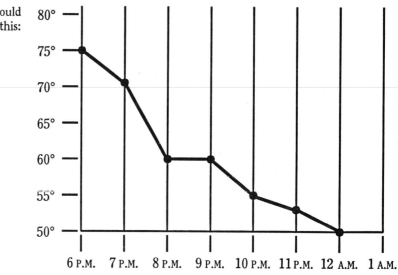

**Pages 42-43**
Questions will vary. Check to see that they are good questions that are based on the clues and picture.
A good answer to the mystery:
Any one of the eyewitnesses could have thrown the tacks on the road causing the bowling ball truck to suffer a flat tire. Only a few could have used the magnet to pull the hinges off the back of the truck just as Harry crossed the street. But only Rachel is named in the last sentence of *Moby Dick*. The last sentence of the Epilogue contains the phrase "It was Rachel."

**Pages 44-45**
1. 18
2. 3
3. 8
Answers for 4-10 will vary.

**Page 47**
1. Give credit if student writes a few of these: clever, self-centered, conceited, chauvinistic, proud, arrogant, best-looking, handsome
2. without respect
3. his favorite wife
4. by using flattery—complimenting his singing
5. the farmer and his sons
6. by appealing to his vanity
7. to the highest tree
8. the forest

**Page 48**
Answers will vary.

**Page 49**
Summaries will vary.

**Page 50**
Answers will vary.

**Page 51**
Answers will vary.

**Page 52**
1. Author: Lucy Maude Montgomery
Subject: life of an orphan
2. Answers will vary.
3. Author: Ray Bradbury
Subject: science fiction
4. Author: Mark Twain
Subject: adventures of teenage boy
5. Answers will vary.
6. Answers will vary.
7. Author: Jane Austen
Subject: relationships; 18th century
8. Answers will vary.
9. Answers will vary.
10. Answers will vary.
11. Answers will vary.
12. Answers will vary.
13. Author: Charles Dickens
Subject: adventures of an orphan boy
14. Answers will vary.
15. Answers will vary.
16. Author: Madeline L'Engle
Subject: science fiction
17. Answers will vary.
18. Answers will vary.